Our Time
Under God Is Now

TWENTY-FIFTH ANNIVERSARY
BMCR

Our Time Under God Is Now

*Reflections
on Black Methodists
for Church Renewal*

Woodie W. White
GENERAL EDITOR

ABINGDON PRESS
Nashville

OUR TIME UNDER GOD IS NOW

ISBN 0-687-29776-1

93 94 95 96 97 98 99 00 01 02—10 9 8 7 6 5 4 3 2 1

MANUFACTURED IN THE UNITED STATES OF AMERICA

Dedicated
in profound appreciation
to those who in a special sense
led the way.

And to those still leading:

Bishop Woodie W. White (Elected 1984)
Indiana Area
General Editor

CONTENTS

INTRODUCTION

Bishop Woodie W. White

It was July 1967. I was attending the jurisdictional conference of the Central Jurisdiction in Nashville, Tennessee. The election of a bishop would, in all likelihood, be the last time the all-Black jurisdictional conference would elect a bishop. The pending union of The Methodist Church and The Evangelical United Brethren Church, creating a new denomination, was expected not to continue a racially structured organizational conference.

I was still a neophyte to church politics and did not have a long history and involvement in the Central Jurisdiction. However, I knew the significance of this historical moment and wanted to be present for this history-making conference. Dr. L. Scott Allen was elected bishop and thus became the last bishop elected by the Central Jurisdictional Conference.

I began to sense the ambivalence of the moment and the times. Since the racially structured Central Jurisdiction was created in 1939 by the merger of The Methodist Episcopal Church, The Methodist Episcopal Church South, and The Methodist Protestant Church, it had been a source of controversy in the denomination. Its creation was nearly unanimously opposed by Black Methodists!

Once the Central Jurisdiction was created, Black Methodists endeavored to make it an effective organization. It became almost a church within a church. Its episcopal leaders were outstanding and effective and highly revered. Both clergy and lay leadership developed and provided leadership for the whole denomination. Lifelong friendships were formed across annual conference lines. The Central Jurisdiction became both beloved and a source of contention and embarrassment. It was still a racially segregated structure! The vast majority of lay and clergy, Black and white, opposed what had become, for all practical purposes, a racially segregated denomination.

However, in the late 1960s, and especially in 1967 and 1968, the growing mood of what one pastor called "creative separatism" was emerging. Black Power, Black Separatism, the Black Movement, became familiar slogans both inside and outside the church. In a sense, what The Methodist Church was working toward, racial integration, was becoming out of vogue in many circles. Yet it was clear that this long-sought goal would not be abandoned despite the appearance that it seemed out of touch with the mood of many Black Americans.

While there was still a commitment to a racially inclusive denomination among the majority of Black Methodists, a growing anxiety and distrust among some had to be addressed. How would the Black laity and clergy be treated in predominantly white annual conferences? Would there be black district superintendents and other staff personnel? Could black elders be elected to the episcopacy in an overwhelmingly white jurisdictional structure? How would fellowship and friendships be maintained as merger scattered annual conferences throughout five jurisdictional conferences? These and other questions were being raised by Black Methodists.

It was during this period the "Black caucus" phenomenon emerged. In predominantly white denominations some Black leaders formed an "unofficial" black caucus to address concerns and advocate for a "Black agenda" in the denomination. Black caucuses had already been organized in at least two denominations when I had my first discussion about such a caucus within the then Methodist Church.

In the summer of 1967, conversations were held with the Reverend James Lawson, then of Memphis; Dr. Negail Riley, recently appointed to the staff of the Board of Missions; the Reverend Marshall Hodge, who was in a "special appointment" in Chicago; the Reverend Gilbert Caldwell of Boston; and Ms. Minnie Stein, staff of the Board of Missions.

As we talked about the possibility of some kind of organization that would address concerns, advocate for certain positions, and provide for fellowship among Black Methodists in the anticipated merged conference, it became clear that we should make some organized effort to determine how much support such a "revolutionary" idea would find.

I remember many of us saying, "Let's check it out with Bishop Golden." Bishop Charles Golden was, for many of us at that time, the bishop with whom we felt easy access. He was gifted, outspoken, and had a good sense of church politics. He would give us sound advice, and we trusted him. As individuals and delegations talked to Bishop Golden, we received his support. However, he made it clear everything we did should be to strengthen the inclusiveness of the denomination, that long-elusive goal.

Soon it was determined to hold a meeting in Detroit to discuss these issues and determine the future. I was given the responsibility to make all local arrangements and send out the notices. James Lawson, Minnie Stein, and Negail Riley, with the assistance of others, took responsibility for organizing our on-site agenda and making key contacts across the Church.

The meeting was held in Detroit in the fall of 1967. Approximately thirty persons from across the nation met to assess the future of Black Methodists in a newly merged denomination. There was enthusiasm, concern, and commitment as we gathered.

It was this meeting that made a decision to hold a National Conference of Negro Methodists in March 1968 in Cincinnati. There was great excitement as the stage was being set to create a Black caucus within The United Methodist Church, as the new denomination would be called.

Thus, in March of 1968, the National Conference of Negro Methodists was convened and adjourned as Black Methodists for Church Renewal. Twenty-five years later, some who were involved in those early days and those who more recently have been impacted by the creation of Black Methodists for Church Renewal, reflect and reminisce in these pages. Learn through their experiences, be inspired through their hopes, gain historical perspective through their reflections. Be challenged as they challenge.

During this time when the nation and church are met with new challenges and even an unfinished agenda in the area of racial justice and inclusiveness, words spoken in 1968 by Dr. Ernest Smith, the Associate General Secretary of the General Board of Church and Society, words which later became the motto of BMCR, are as relevant today as when they were uttered twenty-five years ago: "Our time under God is now!"

Our Time
Under God Is Now

CHAPTER 1   The Early Days

James M. Lawson, Jr.

The 1964 General Conference in Pittsburgh showed me again the shame and the glory of The Methodist Church. I saw the Church at its very best: the hundreds of non-delegates who attended expecting racism to be confronted with prophetic zeal and compassion. We gathered in a nearby church to worship and examine the issues. With fear and trembling I gave the keynote address for the standing-room-only gathering. We expected that Conference to truly advance desegregation of the Church and to open up fresh dimensions of the inclusive church. We wanted boldness. I wanted the Conference to adopt the more realistic program of the Committee of Five of the Central Jurisdiction. Besides the prayers and the vigils, some of us wanted to confront the General Conference in some style that would provoke the sort of discussion and realism that could produce serious change.

I also saw my expectations and hopes dashed. As motion after motion from the Committee of Five and other Black delegates were defeated, a few of us were tempted to go on the floor of the Conference and demand a hearing. It belonged to us even if we were not delegates. Others kept talking us out of such action. But when the last effort from the Central Jurisdiction failed, I wept openly outside the hall. Not even Walter Muelder, one of the wiser heads suggesting that confrontation was not the way, could console me. I knew then that Black Methodists needed another vehicle for the renewal of The Methodist Church. I left Pittsburgh with the certain knowledge that nonviolent action and work were necessary.

Along with disappointment, this Conference also generated excitement. A Central West Conference executive and Negail Riley started from Little Rock, picked me up in

Memphis, and we drove to Pittsburgh. We talked the entire distance of the round trip. Central to those many conversations was the future for Black people in The Methodist Church. We recognized that the Central Jurisdiction would be dissolved. We did not think that General Conference was going about it in a fair or Christian fashion. In various ways we were both active in our cities in the larger Black struggle for freedom and justice. We felt that white people in the Church did not know the issues, that even the more liberal people were more interested in "saving face" for the Church than repenting of the sin of racism. We knew that once again Black Methodists were being asked to take the risks and break up our institutions, that the traffic was one way. We also felt that Black Methodists needed to use more daring tactics and strategies of nonviolence.

For us there was very little evidence that The Methodist Church planned to end the Central Jurisdiction with integrity. There was little or no concern for what Black Methodism offered the entire denomination. There was no interest in the transformation of the Church in the process. We returned to our pulpits disappointed in our Church, but determined to help change that perspective.

Such conversations were frequent among a wide range of people: Maceo Pembroke, Charles Golden, Woodie White, Gilbert Caldwell,

Joseph Lowery, Thelma Barnes, Phil Lawson, Harry Gibson, John Hicks, Clarence Nelson, Joe Gibson, Matthew McCollum, Robert Palmer, Willard Williams, and a host of others.

We did not see our Church taking seriously the escalating movement for freedom as symbolized in Martin Luther King, Jr. We knew that the forces of the South lacked the moral courage to encounter that movement. They did not see the movement as *kairos*. They feared the least step that might alienate their white constituents. They were not in dialogue with any of the Black Methodists deeply involved in that movement.

These things were said in an area meeting called by Bishop Golden at Gulfside in late 1960 or the spring of 1961. We talked about our Church and the future. I chaired the Social Concerns group. Thelma Barnes was the secretary. We asked our bishop to take a request to the College of Bishops of the Central Jurisdiction for a special conference on the integregration of the Central Jurisdiction. We also called for The Methodist Church to make racial justice and reconciliation a priority by creating a commission on religion and race. That commission was to take responsibility for desegregating the church and maintaining inclusivity. Our area meeting adopted those proposals, and Bishop Golden presented them to the College of Bishops.

The Central Jurisdiction became the only jurisdiction of the Church that actually gathered its members and sought a common mind about the future and the end of the Central Jurisdiction. In 1964 the Committee of Five had the broad support of the Central Jurisdiction.

Many conversations and feelings converged with the death of Bishop Marquis Lafayette Harris. The decision was made that the Central Jurisdiction should have a final jurisdictional conference for the election of another bishop. Several of us agreed to meet in Nashville during that final conference and discuss our issues. We sat together in the War Memorial auditorium, which I had helped to desegregate. We met at lunch and dinner. We had agreed that in Nashville we would take action. Negail and Dr. Maceo Pembroke were in that small group. I was there. We agreed that we must call a larger group of people together. We listed the names of people. We set a November date for a weekend workshop in Detroit. We planned a letter and phone calls. We shared our plans with Bishop Golden, who agreed to attend but not to preside. I was asked to chair our conversations and the November meeting.

We rapidly organized and worked on our plans. The November weekend brought a few more than thirty people together. By this time Negail was on the staff of the National Division of the Board of Missions. Several of us lent our offices and budgets to the work.

In November we dared to discuss the hardest questions, such as separating from The Methodist Church. Consensus was firm and clear: We wanted to reform and renew The Methodist Church. We did not intend to leave.

We spent about half of that weekend discussing the full range of issues. Then we came to the mind that a much larger conference of Black Methodists must be called. We did not see any other group that would call such a gathering. The Committee of Five was dissolved. The bishops of the now dissolving Central Jurisdiction could not and would not if asked. So the Detroit gathering sent out a call to others. We set the dates of this first meeting of BMCR for February 6-8, 1968, in Cincinnati. We determined that this larger event would be a working conference. Every person who came would have the chance to express his or her views around three questions: Where are we in The Methodist Church today? What do we want for the whole Church? How do we move in that direction? This continues to be the thrust of BMCR today.

Other than worship, we minimized speeches. We invited Stokeley Carmichael and heard his address. We divided into small groups whose reports were received by a steering committee that pored over all the reports night and day, hammering out our conference report.

(l. to r.) Cain H. Flelder, first executive director of BMCR; Richard (Dick) Lawrence, member of the board of directors; Thelma P. Barnes, associate director. Fifth annual meeting, Philadelphia, 1972.

(PHOTO COURTESY OF THELMA P. BARNES)

That Cincinnati meeting caused hysteria in our Church. We were denounced roundly. Some Black bishops and leaders advised Black Methodists not to attend. At least one bishop wrote a letter to all his pastors telling them not to attend. We were accused of dividing The Methodist Church.

But the conference was a remarkable expression of the Spirit. We worked around the clock without getting weary. We were led into a course of action, a document, a temporary organization, and an immediate strategy for impacting the Church. We knew that Black Methodism had much to offer the whole Church. We voted to attend the Dallas General Conference with a program. We planned to confront that Conference. I was asked to be the temporary chair. I do not remember all the people, but clearly Negail Riley, Woodie White, Maceo Pembroke, and Gil Caldwell were the influential voices giving directions, lifting keen insights, and urging us forward. There were shouting-match issues, such as whether white Methodists should be allowed to belong. But we knew that we were led.

A disciplined group from BMCR attended the Dallas General Conference. Only a handful of our members were delegates. But we did have a plan for making an impact, pushing The Methodist Church and the soon-to-be United Methodist Church toward the Promised Land.

The BMCR initiated a walk-out from the opening Communion service that shook the Church. Yes, there was outrage. The symbolic meaning of the walk-out stirred the conscience and heart of many delegates. We simply said that the Lord's Table was already fractured by racism and the pharaoh-like heart of too much of the Church.

We had also determined to ask Dallas to establish a Commission on Religion and Race, a proposal rejected by the General Conference in 1964. I recall the hectic strategy on Monday evening of the first week. BMCR was repeatedly told that the mood of the Conference was negative toward any progressive forces and that we should not even try to submit our proposals. We, the key leaders of BMCR, including Negail

Riley, Woodie White, and Maceo Pembroke, insisted that we had to be faithful to our God-given and BMCR-affirmed task. I had the material from the Committee of Five. We found a typewriter, and I actually drafted the substitute motion calling for the creation of the Commission on Religion and Race as a new agency with staff. We had decided to make. I think that Woodie White or Negail Riley had made contact with Roy Nichols, then of Oakland, California, and a delegate. He agreed to make our motion. We had decided that when the Inter-Jurisdictional Committee made its report, we would have the substitute motion ready.

I recall our delegation (Negail, Woodie, and I) going to Roy's hotel room much later that Monday night. We handed him our motion and talked briefly with him about it.

I shall never forget the next day. Immediately after Charles Parlin made the report, Roy Nichols was recognized and made his motion. I could feel the Spirit moving through that plenary body. Roy's apology for the motion was simply magnificent. He preached the gospel of Christ Jesus in a faithful, relevant manner. The motion called for the establishment of a general Commission on Religion and Race that would replace the InterJurisdictional Commission and move the UMC toward an inclusive fellowship and mission base. This motion was greeted with standing applause.

(l. to r.) Gilbert H. Caldwell and Maceo D. Pembroke, board chairs; Thelma P. Barnes, second executive director; Cain H. Felder, first executive director; Clayton E. Hammond, board chair. Tenth annual meeting, Little Rock.

(PHOTO COURTESY OF THELMA P. BARNES)

BMCR wanted to penetrate the segregation and racism of the Publishing House. Again from some delegates and others we were advised that the General Conference treated the Publishing House and its president as an entity beyond their influence. We enlisted the talents of Ohio state senator John Bowen of Columbus. The senator was relentless in his cross-examination of Mr. Pierce. The General Conference actually gasped as it learned things about our Publishing House no one had ever asked. In that plenary session the movement began within the General Conference to reform the Publishing House and make it amenable to the General Conference.

We were also surprised that some of the presidents of our Black Methodist-related colleges did not support our overtures to the General Conference for general Church support funds for those colleges. Apparently they somehow were surprised that BMCR was also concerned for those colleges and had them as a priority.

Dallas was another exciting encounter with the Spirit. As a consequence that General Conference decided to hold another General Conference in two years, 1970, rather than waiting until 1972.

From the very first, our BMCR movement tried to be a Spirit-led affair. Wanting the UMC to become inclusive, we set guidelines that meant the officers and board of

BMCR would represent all segments of the nation and Black Methodists. We structured in representation from all five jurisdictions, from laypeople and seminary students. We made certain that lay and clergy were a team. While trying to influence the denomination, we shaped our Constitution and by-laws, we met as a board to set policy and practice, we hired staff, and we raised money, including grants from general Church agencies.

Negail Riley recommended Cain Felder as our first executive director. Cain was just completing seminary at Union in New York. It took courage for him to decide to work for an upstart BMCR. That was a grave risk. BMCR was being seen as radical, separatist. We had trampled upon the good race relations in Methodism. Not even the positive response of the Dallas General Conference calmed the fears that some people held. Cain brought a first-class mind, high competence, zeal for the truth, and enthusiasm coupled with energy. His work helped keep BMCR moving in the right direction.

We confronted the Publishing House with a picket line. Even today in Nashville, I meet employees of the Publishing House who thank me for improving their job situation and opening up new opportunities. Some have told me that they had jobs with the Publishing House because of me.

We challenged the Board of Missions and the Board of Education, insisting that they were essentially racist institutions and had to face that reality.

Through the 1970 General Conference, we saw the Minority Group Self-determination Fund established to be administered by the General Commission on Religion and Race. The Black College Fund was adopted in St. Louis. It was an apportioned fund. It brought to the UMC that the southern conferences should not become the sole support of these colleges. That was one of the issues that some southerners recognized as a barrier to desegregation. BMCR also made the point that these colleges were long neglected by the denomination.

I spent some days with our Hispanic sisters and brothers who wanted to know the BMCR story in order to create their caucus.

BMCR under Negail Riley's leadership proposed to the Board of Missions the Community Developers Program.

By the fall of 1968 Woodie White had become the first general secretary for the new General Commission on Religion and Race. That was BMCR's first major loss of its skilled people. Woodie, of course, remained highly influential for the entire movement and for BMCR behind the scenes. The Commission early adopted a position of financially supporting the development of "people of color" caucuses. That policy greatly blessed BMCR.

The other most influential people were Maceo Pembroke and Negail Riley. Maceo was a very large man with a large vision of the Kingdom. He brought us years of experience across the church. Actually, since I grew up in the Lexington Conference we had been colleagues and friends back into the 1940s. For two terms I served as the president of the Lexington Conference MYF. Maceo was conference director of youth. He became one of the people who advised me. I could always talk to Maceo about everything. It was not an accident that he was in Nashville in August 1967. He was a man about the business of making the Church live up to our high calling.

Negail had the audacity to be a member of the general staff of the Church and yet identify his agenda and God's agenda with the future of Black Methodism. He felt that the UMC could never be faithful to Christ without fully embracing Black Methodists and the gospel we symbolized. He knew that the UMC could only be enriched beyond its imagination if it claimed all its people and felt empowered for mission and ministry among the long neglected. Negail held a vision for BMCR. The vision had an impact on all of us. He influenced BMCR in theology, analysis, structures, money, and programs.

(l. to r.) Thelma P. Barnes, executive director; Maceo D. Pembroke, board chairman; Marie S. McFarland, member of the board of directors, receiving plaque for outstanding leadership in membership development. Eleventh annual meeting.

(ANKERS CAPITOL PHOTOGRAPHERS; PHOTO COURTESY OF THELMA P. BARNES)

In our often hectic national conventions and board meetings, Negail often proposed the compromise that enabled BMCR to take another step in the right direction. I was often the presiding officer and relished his interventions, which allowed the meeting to move on.

In those first years BMCR helped to shape the agenda of the UMC. We brought a spirit of renewal and transformation. We made racism, desegregation, justice, and freedom issues for the church. We challenged the denomination to stretch toward its very being as God's people. We dared to love the Church enough to confront her sin and work for her sanctification. We dared to be Black and followers of Jesus and Methodists.

CHAPTER 2

BMCR:
Its Reasons

Gilbert H. Caldwell

Black Methodists for Church Renewal was organized in 1968 because many Black Methodists were concerned about these realities as we moved toward the 1968 union between The Methodist Church and Evangelical United Brethren: (1) absorption, (2) advocacy, (3) invisibility, (4) powerlessness, and (5) renewal.

(1) Absorption. Even as the Central Jurisdiction was being merged/dissolved, many of us were concerned that our history, our cultural experience, and the uniqueness of our particular pilgrimage as displaced Africans would be ignored or lost forever.

One writer has stated that sometimes "we do the right things for the wrong reasons." As then Negro Methodists, we were not sure that the efforts directed toward merger were being carried out for the right reasons. We were not sure that the

motivation for merger represented authentic commitment to a receiving of the spirituality, culture, and creative organizational practices of African-American Methodists.

Thus Black Methodists for Church Renewal was born!

(2) Advocacy. We knew then, as we know now, that the best advocates for the people are the people themselves. Those who know and have lived the history of exclusion, those who have practiced the arts of racial survival, are their own best advocates.

We knew that any progress ever made by African Americans was made because they themselves questioned, challenged, confronted, protested, and helped to reshape policies and practices that dehumanized, excluded, and repressed them. These protest actions were necessary because of the terrible legacy of slavery, segregation, separation, discrimination, and the powerlessness that

Gilbert Caldwell.

(PHOTO COURTESY OF JOHN COLEMAN)

(l. to r.) Earl Wilson, Doug Fitch, Woodie White, Mary Goode, Thelma Barnes, Gilbert Caldwell. Annual meeting, Chicago, 1989.

(PHOTO COURTESY OF JOHN COLEMAN)

26

accompanied each of these experiences. There were African Americans then and there are African Americans today who have not yet acknowledged, or understood, our peculiar American racial history. We must constantly remind ourselves and others of our history—both the positive and the less than positive history.

So, out of a deep realization of the necessity for advocacy, Black Methodists for Church Renewal was born!

(3) Invisibility. It is so easy for a people who have been separated and segregated because of their color to become invisible despite their colorfulness. "Out of sight, out of mind!" Some persons were concerned that merger would remove African Americans, with all of our variety of distinctive skin colors, from visibility in the mind, life, and practices of a denomination in which we were and are a numerical minority.

Coupled with a concern for invisibility was a recognition that institutions have the capacity to declare of certain segments of the population that they can be seen, but not heard. We were concerned that we would not only experience a psychological kind of invisibility in a merged church, but that our voices would be unheard, unheeded, and silenced.

Thus Black Methodists for Church Renewal was born!

(4) Powerlessness. Power is the capacity to make sure that a particular perspective of a person or group of persons will be taken seriously. In 1967, we recognized the reality of, and the necessity for, power and the capacity to influence that results from power. We understood that we could not depend on others to use their influence on our behalf when we had no influence ourselves.

Our painful and negative history in this land, and within the institutions of this land (particularly the church), would not and could not have occurred if "good people" had not used scripture, conformity to cultural folkways and mores, and silent consent to subjugate a people. We knew from our history and our experience that even "good people" were reluctant to use their power to empower African Americans.

Thus Black Methodists for Church Renewal was born!

(5) Renewal. We deliberately chose to include renewal in our name because we knew that a church that was so much a captive of culture that, in its institutional life it reflected the exclusive, unfair, restrictive, and separatist political and economic practices of the nation, needed renewal!

Merger without renewal would not reflect the biblical faith, the call to mission and evangelism, and the God-directed distinctiveness that the Church claims. Black Methodists for Church Renewal believed and hopefully still believes that African-American Methodists did not consent to merger without renewal. It is our understanding that God is constantly making all things new. That has sustained us as we have responded to the renewal that comes from saying yes to Jesus Christ. We know that we cannot expect our denomination to be renewed if we, as Black United Methodists, are not renewed.

Black Methodists for Church Renewal was not founded as a separatist or anti-white organization. We knew then, as we know now, that God is not finished with any of us yet. Therefore, we came into being because we believed in God's hope for all of us. We knew that United Methodism could never be the Church it felt God wanted it to be if people of African descent failed to express and share the dignity that comes only from God.

Thus, out of a concern about absorption, advocacy, invisibility, powerlessness, and renewal, Black Methodists for Church Renewal was born!

CHAPTER 3   Through the Years

Thelma P. Barnes

On February 6-9, 1968, in Cincinnati, Ohio, the National Conference of Negro Methodists convened with 259 registered delegates from every geographical jurisdiction in Methodism. This conference, called by an ad hoc committee of more than 100 members, was attended by persons who responded to an invitation to participate in developing "a life of power and unity in the new United Methodist Church."

During this meeting we looked at the new situation before us in The Methodist Church; we explored strategies for helping The United Methodist Church to really become effective on the local level through annual conferences, boards and agencies, jurisdictional conferences, and the General Conference.

Seventeen work groups assembled to discuss, plan, and bring recommendations to the plenary regarding the role of the local church; what annual conferences and districts must do to free Black Methodist churches for ministry to black communities; what boards and agencies in the Church must do; and relevant legislation and strategy for General Conference.

A review of the staffing of general boards and agencies revealed limited representation of Negroes employed with professional status, a total of twenty-two at that time.

The plight of the Negro Colleges was a major concern. Civil rights, social and economic justice, peace, and general welfare were items that needed to be addressed by the local church.

The findings of the conference revealed that we needed to consider the recruitment and itineracy of the Negro pastors to lift up the distinctive mission that the Black church can and must carry into the "new" Church; to propose urgent priority missions for the cities where we live; to suggest new forms for the life of

(l. to r.) Joseph E. Lowery, banquet speaker; Hugh Dash, executive director, Enterprises Now, Inc.; Thelma P. Barnes. Eleventh anual meeting.

(ANKERS CAPITOL PHOTOGRAPHERS; PHOTO COURTESY OF THELMA P. BARNES)

BMCR Youth Conference.

(PHOTO COURTESY OF JOHN COLEMAN)

the local congregation; and to precipitate creative motives for the kind of unity among Negro Methodists that could mean a vigorous, faithful Methodism.

The findings also noted the need to increase the representation of Blacks at the professional staff level of the general boards and agencies to increase adequate representation in policy-making positions. It was noted that improvements needed to be made in Black representation on the board of trustees of the various Methodist colleges. Since we were entering a new relationship, which we hoped would be truly inclusive, it was felt that all hospitals, homes, community centers, residences, and agencies under the auspices of the Church should cease all forms of racial segregation and discrimination in their admission policies and practices.

As for us in attendance, we affirmed the search for Black identity, knowing that if we were obedient to God's creation we had a responsibility to ourselves, to the white community, and to white Methodists to relate from a position of power. We affirmed our belief in God and his church, acknowledging that all men and women are brothers and sisters in Christ.

We discussed the role of the local church, including: principles regarding local church staffing and financing; the local church and Black culture; our response to the local church community; effective educational programming; the local church and creative power; the local church and economic independence.

General legislative proposals were developed where required to ensure implementation of some of the recommendations for presentation to the 1968 General Conference.

After reviewing and discussing recommendations from each of the seventeen work groups, it was decided that an ongoing ad hoc structure would be needed to begin implementing the findings of the conference. The findings were adopted with an overwhelming consensus.

The name of the organization would be Black Methodists for Church Renewal (BMCR). It was interesting to note that we entered the conference as "Negro" Methodists and emerged at the end of the conference as "Black" Methodists. We took a good look at ourselves as Black men and women, reclaimed our heritage, and came out of that meeting as Black persons unashamed.

A national board of directors was elected with James M. Lawson elected to serve as chairman. This board consisted of 44 persons. Regional convenors were elected for the five geographic jurisdictions. A budget was established. We voted to elect an executive director when sufficient funds were secured to cover three years' operation.

(l. to r.) Hugh Dash; Thelma P. Barnes.

(PHOTO COURTESY OF THELMA P. BARNES)

BMCR Youth Conference.

(PHOTO COURTESY OF JOHN COLEMAN)

The following persons were elected as members of the board of directors: James M. Lawson, Chairman; Frederick Arnold; Thelma P. Barnes; Harold L. Bell; Gilbert Caldwell; Ernestine Cofield; George Daniels; Fannie Dorsey; Douglass Fitch; T. F. Frierson; Joseph Gibson; Mary Good; Clayton Hammond; Richard Hicks; Kenneth Holley; Zan Holmes, Jr.; Frank Horton; William Jason; Charles Kellogg; Merrill Lindsey; Joseph Lowery; Robert McClain; Marie McFarland; James McRee; E. A. Mayes; Roy Neal; Randolph Nugent; Robert J. Palmer; Archie Rich; Negail Riley; Anthony Shipley; C. Jasper Smith; Cornelia L. Smith; Howard Spencer; Marion Spencer; Minnie Stein; Melvin Talbert; William J. Washington; Woodie White; A. Cecil Williams; Frank Williams; Willard Williams; W. Earle Wilson; and Samuel Wright.

Regional convenors elected were: Western—Douglass Fitch; North Central—Woodie White; Northeastern—Randolph Nugent; South Central—William J. Washington; Southeastern—C. Jasper Smith. They were elected for the purpose of convening the initial regional meeting in the respective jurisdictions.

Inclusiveness was a major consideration in developing the guidelines for operation. The Constitution and by-laws mandated that if the executive director were a male, the associate director would be a female, and vice versa. It provided for proportionate clergy and lay membership on the board of directors and also for youth and young adult representation. Persons were elected to three-year terms and were required to be off the board for at least one year before being eligible for re-election.

As time progressed women's and men's concerns groups were organized, and a youth component was organized at the national level.

Funding was to be pursued from the following sources: The United Methodist Church boards, agencies, annual conferences, and other church structures; foundations; other denominations; councils of Churches; membership fees; individuals (one percent of personal income); churches (a portion of the church's apportionments and benevolence giving); Black churches ("free-will" offering).

The national annual meetings are always a highlight of the organization. It is a learning, fellowship time. The organization has been blessed with outstanding leadership during these meetings through its workshop leaders, keynote speakers, planners, committee and task force chairpersons and members, youth and young adult leaders, supporters of men's and women's concerns and leaders in local churches.

Some of the major achievements of the National Black Methodists for Church Renewal through 1980 were:
1. Organized a national forum for

33

Black United Methodist leadership to assess the implications of phasing out the Central Jurisdiction in light of the critical need for Black empowerment.

2. Lobbied effectively at the 1968 General Conference to create the Commission on Religion and Race of The United Methodist Church.

3. Joined with other agencies to sponsor the Black Community Developers Program of The United Methodist Church.

4. Held major demonstrations at Methodist agencies to increase the denomination's participation in the national equal employment program called Project Equality.

5. Urged the various agencies of The United Methodist Church to upgrade significantly the level of Black leadership in the areas of responsibility throughout the church.

6. Brought the 1970 General Conference to the point of creating a $2,000,000 per year social development fund for Black people and other minorities.

7. Secured a General Conference commitment to raise $4,000,000 per year for the Black Methodist Colleges and their students.

8. Launched several projects of national significance for Black Methodists, such as Enterprises Now (MESBIC), an investment and lending assistance program for Black businesses; an aftercare and drug abuse treatment center; and a documentary film on the Black church.

9. Created a significant number of local caucuses within various annual conferences of The United Methodist Church, consistent with the national theme of constituency building.

10. Published a national newspaper, with a readership of more than six thousand, and several books and resource materials for Black Methodists planning for community action at the local level.

11. Increased the level of investing in Black enterprises and banks by agencies of The United Methodist Church.

The national office of BMCR experienced many staff variations. It has operated with as many as four full-time staff persons and two student interns, and as few as two full-time staff persons and temporary part-time help. The office staff provided on-the-job training for one full-time administrative secretary; supervised training for two students in the area of bookkeeping; two students in general office work (Atlanta Urban Corps Summer Program); and a total of sixteen student interns from Clark College (two in general office and fourteen in journalism).

We recruited three church and community workers and in cooperation with the National Board of Global Ministries expanded the

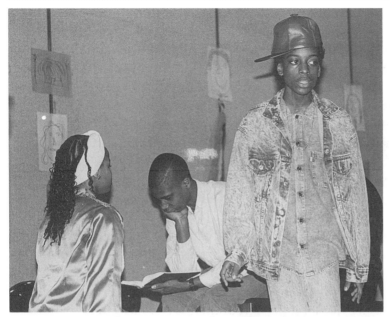

BMCR Youth Conference.   *(PHOTO COURTESY OF JOHN COLEMAN)*

BMCR Youth Conference.
    (PHOTO COURTESY OF JOHN COLEMAN)

national staff. One worker was assigned to assist with NOW, the national newspaper, and public relations for BMCR; one worker was assigned to serve as the resource person in the area of local church training, to coordinate the work of the BMCR National Youth Network, and to assist with administrative functions; one worker was assigned to specialize in the area of hunger and assist with the development of a model center for social change.

Limited funding throughout many years of operation demanded hard work and creativity by staff persons to ensure survival. Special mention must be made of several persons who made personal sacrifices and remained committed to their tasks. They are: Lillian Williams, Madelyn Greene, Cecilia Morris-Lyons, and Newtonia Harris Coleman.

Space is not available to list the names of the many persons who served faithfully on the national BMCR board of directors and throughout the jurisdictions.

Many outstanding national leaders have addressed the organization at its annual national meetings.

National staff persons serving The United Methodist Church have been supportive and helpful in providing leadership in a variety of ways. Persons serving on the boards and agencies, from conference to national level, have been helpful in supporting the BMCR agenda. The United Methodist Church can boast of a richer heritage having had a BMCR along the way.

CHAPTER 4

How BMCR Has Helped United Methodism Move Toward Renewal

John G. Corry

Article IV, Division I, of the Constitution of The United Methodist Church states:

The United Methodist Church is part of the Church Universal, which is one Body in Christ. Therefore all persons, without regard to race, color, national origin, or economic condition, shall be eligible to attend its worship services, to participate in its programs, and, when they take the appropriate vows, to be admitted into its membership in any local church in the connection. In The United Methodist Church no conference or other organizational unit of the Church shall be structured so as to exclude any member or any constituent body of the Church because of race, color, national origin, or economic condition.

The United Methodist Church has not to date lived up to this constitutional mandate. It was anticipated by Black Methodists for Church Renewal that the Church would have to be prodded and coerced into living up to this provision. With this anticipation Black Methodists for Church Renewal, Inc. set out in its Constitution and By-Laws, Article II, as one of its purposes this provision: "To act as an agitating conscience on all boards and agencies of The United Methodist Church in order to keep them sensitive to the needs and expressions of a genuinely *inclusive* relevant church [emphasis added]." The organization later expanded this thrust to include every organizational entity and programmatic emphasis within the Church.

One of the most notable efforts of inter-ethnic cooperation occurred leading up to the 1984 General Conference when the various ethnic caucuses coalesced to move the Church toward inclusiveness. The various ethnic caucuses, including Black Methodists for Church Renewal, felt that continuing to develop and strengthen the ethnic minority local churches for another quadrennium (1985–88) was one way of increasing and ensuring equity and inclusiveness in United Methodism. The General Council on Ministries felt that

priority had run its course and recommended another missional priority for the 1985–88 quadrennium.
Spearheaded by Black Methodists
for Church Renewal, an Inter-Ethnic
Strategy Development Committee
was created to formulate, write, and
circulate its own missional priority.
Representatives to that group in-
cluded the following:

*Black Methodists for Church Renewal
(BMCR)*
Betty Henderson, Carolyn Ander-
son, and John G. Corry

*Metodistas Asociados Representando
la Causa de Hispanos Americanos
(MARCHA)*
José Palos, German Acevedo, Joel
Martinez (now bishop), and Dalila
Cruz

*Native American International Cau-
cus (NAIC)*
Marvin Abrams, Cynthia Abrams,
and Homer Noley

*National Federation of Asian Ameri-
can United Methodists (NFAAUM)*
Roy Sano (now bishop), Peter Y. K.
Sun, Naomi Southard, and Leo Hsu

Resource persons from the various
general boards and agencies in-
cluded the late C. Leonard Miller,
Douglass E. Fitch, David White, Eli
Rivera, Yolando Pupo-Ortiz, and
Manuel C. Espartero.
The above group of persons set

about the task of developing the
missional priority, writing the document, devising ways and means for
its distribution to the Council of
Bishops, General Conference delegates, members of the various general boards and agencies, and other
interested persons. The theme
selected for the proposed missional
priority was "Developing and
Strengthening the Ethnic Minority
Local Church for Witness and Mission."
Having written and distributed
the document, this group faced the
formidable task of trying to convince
the delegates to General Conference
to vote for the missional priority
proposed by the Inter-Ethnic Caucus
rather than the one recommended
by the General Council on Ministries. Black Methodists for Church
Renewal chose John G. Corry to
coordinate its effort in this direction
at the General Conference in Balti-
more in 1984. He was ultimately
selected by the Inter-Ethnic Caucus
to coordinate the strategies there for
that group. With a group of dedicated persons, he and they went
about the task of devising ways to
contact and influence General Conference delegates in every annual
conference. The ultimate result was
that when the vote was taken on the
floor of General Conference, to the
surprise of so many who said the
proposal from the Inter-Ethnic Caucus didn't have a chance of acceptance, that proposal prevailed as the

one adopted by the General Conference.

The above anecdote illustrates one way in which National Black Methodists for Church Renewal has impacted United Methodism in its efforts to move toward genuine inclusiveness. Efforts are also being made by jurisdictional and conference caucuses all across the Church to move the Church toward inclusiveness. The caucuses have challenged leadership at every level of the Church to live up to our constitutional mandate of inclusiveness. Our work, however, is not done until we become a truly and genuinely inclusive Church!

Leonard Miller.
(PHOTO COURTESY OF JOHN COLEMAN)

CHAPTER 5   An Agent of Change

George M. Daniels

The United Methodist Church has undergone cataclysmic changes in the twenty-five years since the birth of Black Methodists for Church Renewal. Prior to 1968, every general program board of The Methodist Church was drowning in racism.

An example is the General Board of Global Ministries, where I spent twenty-eight years as a writer and editor. There were only three Black executives at Global Ministries when I arrived there in 1961. Of more than fifteen hundred missionaries serving overseas in Africa, Asia, and Latin America, fewer than twenty were Black. It was only in 1967 that an unwritten "blockade" against Black executives in the Board's World Program Division was broken with the hiring of a Black woman. But as late as 1969, a year after BMCR was founded, two white missionaries were still directing mission work for all of Africa, the Middle East, and Europe.

However, unlike some agencies of the Church, there were vigorous internal struggles taking place that ultimately led to the hiring of more Black Americans, women, Hispanics, Asians, and Native Americans. These struggles also led to revolutionary programmatic changes that have since created a mission agency that many years ago could have existed only in the dreams of those Black preachers and lay men and women who preceded us.

A leader in these struggles was Dr. Negail R. Riley, a Black executive of Global Ministries' National Program Division from 1966 until his death in 1987 at the age of 57. Largely through his work, BMCR was born to provide the specific ministries that would address these issues. The rest is history.

BMCR has assisted Black local churches in becoming more responsive to the needs of their members and communities by pressuring gen-

Members of choir from Los Angeles. Annual meeting, Las Vegas, 1992.

(PHOTO COURTESY OF JOHN COLEMAN)

eral program agencies to commit greater financial resources to Black churches and by persuading them to hire more ethnic minority personnel on their staffs.

BMCR has made its presence felt from the beginning and has matured into one of the most effective agents of change in our time. To its credit, it has helped in no small way to create the Church we have today.

Member of choir from Los Angeles. Annual meeting, Las Vegas, 1992.

(PHOTO COURTESY OF JOHN COLEMAN)

CHAPTER 6

Black and United Methodist

Zan W. Holmes

One of the most liberating events that I have experienced as a United Methodist minister occurred in the fall of 1967 in Detroit. On this occasion I had the privilege of participating in a historic meeting of a small group of Black Methodist ministers and laypersons who made plans for the eventual formation of Black Methodists for Church Renewal.

Since its formation, BMCR has become a major liberating experience for Methodism in general. But primarily, BMCR has been a significant liberating experience for United Methodism's Black constituency.

Indeed, as I see it, BMCR's major message to United Methodism's Black constituency is: By the grace of God, we can be Black and United Methodist too! In other words, BMCR helped us realize that we do not have to make a choice between our Blackness and United Methodism. Indeed, BMCR has helped us

proclaim that it is when we are most authentically ourselves and claim our God-given heritage that we make our best contribution to The United Methodist Church, for the sake of the gospel. Black people often identify with this theme of liberating self-affirmation as portrayed in the story of David the shepherd boy in his battle with the giant Goliath as recorded in the biblical book of I Samuel. Judging from all outward circumstances, it appeared that little David did not have much of a chance to win. After all, he was a youth and small of stature, whereas the giant Goliath was much greater in stature and more sophisticated and experienced in the art of battle. Yet in spite of the vast differences between the two of them, the battle was miraculously won by little David, the underdog. And I believe that the turning point that ensured victory for David on behalf of Israel was his decision to be his God-given self.

At first David was clothed with the armor of King Saul. But the king's clothes did not fit David properly. In fact, if David had worn them he would have felt uncomfortable and unnatural. Because they were clothes that did not fit, they would have been more of a handicap than an asset and would have made David awkward and ineffective in the battle. Therefore, it was a significant liberating decision when David said to King Saul, "I cannot walk with these; for I am not used to them" (I Samuel 17:39). Instead, he took them off, put on his own clothes, and took up his trusty and reliable slingshot with which he was familiar. In other words, he was saying: "I gotta be me." Thus he went out to win a vital victory not only for himself, but for the whole nation of Israel.

BMCR has encouraged and enabled the Black constituency of The United Methodist Church to say, by the grace of God, "I gotta be me." Thus, we have won victories not only for ourselves, but for all of United Methodism.

For example, the *Songs of Zion* hymnbook was influenced by BMCR. Under the leadership of Dr. William McClain it was shaped and directed by an advisory task force of Black United Methodists who were liberated by the grace of God and enabled to say, "I gotta be me." Thus, The United Methodist Church has a songbook out of the Black tradition that has become a blessing not only to Black people, but to United Methodism in general and to many other Christians.

Likewise, predominantly Black congregations that are growing the fastest in our denomination are churches that are Black and Methodist too! This is the legacy of BMCR. A notable example is the Windsor Village United Methodist Church in Houston, Texas. Indeed it is not only our fastest growing predominantly Black church, but one of the fastest growing churches in all United Methodism, with a membership approaching six thousand in its first ten years of existence.

This is significant when measured against the backdrop of the civil rights struggle of the sixties and the continuing struggle for justice in the midst of the continuing injustices in our society and in the church today. This has produced a climate in which many Black people have become disenchanted with and disaffected from all institutions, including the church. To be sure, in a day when many young Black people are reclaiming their African heritage, they are often tempted by alien voices who claim that Christianity is the "white man's religion." In this climate BMCR has been an effective agent of evangelism with its counter-claim that we do not have to surrender our African heritage in order to be United Methodist and Christian. BMCR has reminded us that Black people were present at the very inception of Methodism in America. BMCR has reminded us that there is an African presence in the Bible. BMCR has helped us embrace the fullness of our African connection.

Indeed, BMCR has reminded us that "in Christ there is no east or west, in him no south or north; but one great fellowship of love throughout the whole wide earth."

Finally, BMCR exists as an ongoing reminder to United Methodism that our journey toward racial and ethnic inclusiveness is an unfinished agenda. Even though we have come a mighty long way, we still have a mighty long way to go. Thus we can never afford the luxury of being satisfied with ourselves as we are. Instead we must ever have a

noble sense of discontent with things as they are in our Church and in society.

One day someone asked an artist what was his greatest painting. Surprisingly he did not point to any painting he had already done. Instead, pointing to the future, he said, "The next one."

As we celebrate twenty-five years of BMCR, I pray that when we are asked to name our greatest year we will not point to the past. Instead, looking ahead to the unfinished agenda before us, may we answer with the artist: "The next one!" And may our theme song be:

We're pressing on the upward way,
New heights we're gaining every day;
Still praying as we're onward bound,
"Lord, plant my feet on higher ground."
  —Johnson Oatman, Jr.

Choir from Los Angeles singing at annual meeting, Las Vegas, 1992.

(PHOTO COURTESY OF JOHN COLEMAN)

CHAPTER 7

The Value of BMCR to the African-American Constituency in United Methodism

Douglass E. Fitch

"If it were not for Black Methodists for Church Renewal, I would still be a single parent, employed in a maintenance position without a college degree, and largely unfulfilled. But because BMCR demanded The United Methodist Church live out its mission of inclusiveness, I got the chance of a lifetime. BMCR inspired me to go to college. I am a parent with a college degree working as a professional in my career of choice in The United Methodist Church. Without fear of contradiction this would not have happened without BMCR!"

The creation of BMCR was both necessary and essential. BMCR assisted African Americans to reconcile their newfound status inside a predominantly white denomination while maintaining their integrity. Politically and culturally, history crossed a new threshold. Black power was a reality! This new current focused on personal esteem and heritage, community empowerment, the development of more relevant Black institutions, and the pulling together of resources to overcome years of oppression. It was critical for African-American constituents at this pivotal juncture in history to state categorically whether they would respond to these new currents inside the denomination or outside of it. BMCR brought together our tradition that affirmed the redeeming power of Jesus Christ and the sustaining, nurturing presence of the Holy Spirit long before the civil rights years; thus God's revelation for us can be expressed in the immortal words of Dr. Ernest Smith: "Our time under God is now." The decision was made to stay in the denomination we helped birth.

BMCR has been helpful in enabling African Americans to struggle with the many forms of racism—personal, institutional, and cultural, at the levels of the general Church, annual conference, jurisdictional conference, district, and local

(l. to r.) Woodie W. White, C. Leonard Miller, Cain H. Felder, Isaac Miller. 1973.

(PHOTO COURTESY OF NATIONAL BMCR, DAYTON)

church. BMCR has kept us balanced and focused for the many tasks before the denomination and African-American constituents. It has been invaluable in enabling so many of us to maintain integrity with the new currents of history while remaining faithful to the demands of the gospel. BMCR has demanded that the general Church fulfill its mission while at the same time keeping African Americans clear about its own particular agenda.

BMCR called forth a new leadership from among African Americans to serve throughout the denomination. It also inspired interest in knowing this new system and how to make it work for us. Thus BMCR protested and addressed injustices but also sought significant positions inside the system in order that African Americans and the general Church might see a visible presence as fruit of its labor.

BMCR has remained clear about the African-American agenda and the agenda of the general Church. Sometimes we have worked on the same agenda, such as historically Black colleges. At other times the general Church has not had the vision or felt the pain of the agenda peculiar to African-American constituents: African-American male extinction, school drop-outs, warehousing of African Americans in penal institutions, and other issues peculiar to us. It has been in the interests of BMCR to keep African-American constituents conscious of our obligations to address these needs—not by ourselves alone but with the assistance of others.

BMCR has been valuable in spawning a new generation of clergy and lay leadership. BMCR initiated in the North Central Jurisdiction programs for clergy and laity. The same has been done with varying degrees of success throughout the other jurisdictions. A network of able leaders has emerged in addition to coalitions that reach beyond our own racial identity. Through BMCR, African-American constituents have set goals and organized, strategized, and implemented numerous projects and programs directly related to our constituents as well as with persons and groups beyond BMCR.

BMCR has enabled many of us to renew the joy we once knew so intimately in the Central Jurisdiction. It has enabled us to keep alive the sense of celebration from our tradition of worship, and to develop worship resources from that tradition for ourselves and the worldwide Christian community. Moreover, it enables us to fellowship annually, critique our work, and commit to God's new revelation for these times.

BMCR has been our bridge over troubled waters. Yet in the very best of our tradition the beneficiaries of this creative, inspired act of God in history are those who reach far beyond BMCR. If there is any passion and compassion among many of us in this new church, we who call ourselves African Americans credit it to BMCR. It taught us how to "sing the Lord's song in a strange land."

Our time under God is still now!

CHAPTER 8   A Personal Perspective

Gilbert H. Caldwell

Black Methodists for Church Renewal for many of us was a response to our participation in the March on Washington in 1963, the "Freedom Summer" of 1964 in Mississippi, and the Selma-to-Montgomery March in 1965. It was also an appropriate response to our pain over the deaths of four girls in a church bombing in Birmingham in 1963, the assassination of Malcolm X in 1965, and the assassination of Martin Luther King, Jr., in 1968. BMCR gave many of us an opportunity to reflect collectively on the events taking place in the middle and at the end of the 1960s.

We could not isolate ourselves as Black Methodists from all that was occurring in the nation and within the communities where we lived. Someone has said that the Christian must live "with the Bible in one hand and the newspaper in the other." We did not want to be victimized by the all-too-common seduction that The Methodist Church was so self-contained and self-sufficient that it did not have to concern itself with domestic struggle. BMCR allowed us to identify with and participate in the struggles and activism of our black brothers and sisters throughout the nation and the world.

But BMCR also challenged us to accept and assume our responsibilities, individually and as a people. The late Howard Thurman, who influenced many of us when he was Dean of Marsh Chapel at Boston University, once wrote: "The great danger an oppressed people risk is to assume that they are exempt from doing the will of God." We could spend so much time focusing our attention on "racist" systems, institutions, and persons that we might avoid our responsibility to be responsible. We knew that if bigoted persons and institutions changed overnight, we still must assume

Worship at annual meeting, Cleveland, 1985.

(PHOTO COURTESY OF NATIONAL BMCR, DAYTON)

responsibility for the integrity, spirituality, and ethicality of our quest for justice and inclusiveness.

Black Methodists for Church Renewal served and serves the purpose of keeping us honest and moral within our personal and communal journeys. Time and time again, as African Americans we have had to grapple with the question: What does it profit us if we gain the whole world and lose our souls?

BMCR in those early days helped us challenge the loneliness of being members of a numerical minority amid a majority. This numerical minority status is heightened when the majority is not convinced of the legitimacy of the humanity of the minority. (My most difficult pastoral calls in my ministry were those when I visited with white persons who stopped participating in their church because I was the new pastor.)

Within BMCR we could really "let go and let God." We could be free to unashamedly and unapologetically focus on our Black history and reality with its joys, sorrows, triumphs, and tribulations. As one of the characters in Alice Walker's *Color Purple* says, "We could celebrate each other."

One of the challenges I faced during my time as National Chairperson of BMCR (1971–74) is descriptive of the ambivalence that is always present for Black persons who believe that it is possible to provide leadership in predominantly white *and* Black institutions and organizations. In 1973 I became pastor of First United Methodist Church in New Haven, Connecticut. Some of my BMCR colleagues felt there was a contradiction in the BMCR elected leader serving as pastor of a predominantly white church. I kidded some of them by saying, "They did not seem to have difficulty with having a Black district superintendent or bishop of a predominantly white district or area." I am not sure that some of my friends accepted this tongue-in-cheek humor.

Nevertheless I contended then, as I contend now, that it is essential that Black persons demonstrate a bold and clear commitment to African-American concerns and interests, particularly within white institutions. Our concerns are the concerns of the total human family. No people are fulfilled as long as another people are limited and restricted. The journey for justice belongs to all of us.

BMCR helped me understand and practice joy and celebration amid the struggle. I had been brought up with the understanding that too much celebration and joy reflected negatively on one's character, education, and sophistication. I was therefore startled when participating in the marches and demonstrations in the South; in the evening many of the participants were able to relax and renew through music and dance and celebration. Many persons who had been assaulted and dehumanized in the action of the day were now able to allow the joy of celebration to energize them for the challenges of the next day. I had been carefully taught the necessity of separating the sacred from the secular. For years I had struggled with my love of jazz and what appeared to be a rejection of this art form by church leadership.

I discovered as I worked and played and prayed with my BMCR colleagues that we do a great disservice to the God who created us by hiding our laughter, joy, and celebration under a bushel. Certainly, restraint and discipline are essential, but if we seek to be "whole" persons, then we must be complete persons. Black people have survived and thrived because we understood the scripture that states: "Weeping may endure for a night, but joy comes in the morning." BMCR has survived for twenty-five years because of the need to challenge consistently racial injustice, but we have been energized by our understanding that "Jesus is the center of our joy."

The United Methodist Church is one of God's significant agents of sharing the Christian gospel of salvation, reconciliation, and liberation. Black Methodists for Church Renewal believes in what God has done and will do with our denomination. In our confrontations, challenges, and cooperative acts, BMCR has expressed its conviction that "God is not finished with [United Methodism] yet."

CHAPTER 9

What BMCR Has Meant to Me

Betty Ann Henderson

Black Methodists for Church Renewal has provided me with innumerable opportunities to be a quiet observer; an active participant; and a spokesperson for the concerns, issues, hopes, and dreams of Black American constituents who call The United Methodist Church home. During my twenty-three-year journey through memory lane (having served as chairperson of a local and jurisdictional caucus, vice chair and chair of the board of directors), I recalled some of the good and bad, the learnings, the disappointments, the challenges, and the opportunities that were before me and the organization early in its existence. Some of these same concerns continue to plague us today.

Early in my education and involvement in this new church (with the dissolution of the Central Jurisdiction), I discovered that things would not always be fair or equitable. It was necessary for

BMCR to strategize, "act up," and sometimes confront the "white" Church, forcing it to do right and be Christian. Not totally prepared for and cognizant of these facts, I quickly began survival training for leadership within the denomination.

In 1970 I was a member of the Youth/Young Adult Task Force of BMCR. My first assignment was to participate in a youth meeting and serve as an observer at the 1970 special session of the General Conference. The Youth/Young Adult task force ended up confronting the Council of Bishops (for not listening to us) by blocking exits to a meeting room. My role as an observer immediately turned into that of an active participant. It became an awesome experience for me, then a very shy and quiet person.

The task force's role was to influence those persons making plans and setting policy for the participation of young people in the life of

Southeast Jurisdiction BMCR Youth Conference, Clark College, Atlanta, 1988.

(PHOTO COURTESY OF JOHN COLEMAN)

the Church. BMCR provided an arena for young Black people to have an active role in the life of the Church and the opportunity to meet and dialogue with leadership throughout the denomination. From this experience, I realized BMCR was a powerful force for change within the Church.

BMCR has afforded me an opportunity to develop leadership skills that are used and (I believe) appreciated throughout the life of the Church. It has offered me the opportunity to challenge those inside as well as outside the life of the organization. BMCR opened doors and gave me exposure to a national and international Church.

In 1978, I was elected coordinator of the Northeastern Jurisdiction for BMCR. This automatically made me a member of the National Board of Directors for BMCR. (I was now playing in the big league!) BMCR provided me with a real education in the life and politics of the Church. BMCR was the arena where programs were developed to educate the Black constituency about the life of the Church. Board members were held accountable for the development of strategy for implementation in their local areas and for the strengthening of caucuses in the annual conferences and the jurisdictions. They were also responsible for the enhancing of Black local churches to be about ministry in "white" annual conferences without losing their Black identity. Individuals and groups were empowered.

BMCR underscored the importance of the Black church's knowing its history, being proud of it, and sharing this history with the larger denomination. BMCR worked closely with the general Church boards and agencies to encourage the hiring of Black leadership in executive-level positions. At this same time the struggle for power and leadership was occurring in the organization. (What happens within religious organizations is just a microcosm of what happens in other types of organizations.)

BMCR was the platform in which any Black person could get a real education about politics in the life of the Church. My experiences were not always pleasant, but such is life. This is not intended as a negative comment, but it is real.

BMCR has served the role of advocate, educator, teacher, trainer servant, frustration bearer, and social activist. Sometimes in our history, BMCR has done an outstanding job; other times, it is not so admirable. The membership and participation at any given time have influenced the leadership and helped to determine the performance. Sometimes we do not want to make changes, are afraid of the appointive process (a reality), have become comfortable and are not willing to share (whatever it is we have) with other sisters and brothers, and are not as trusting of each other as we should be.

Because of some of my earlier learnings and experiences with BMCR, I have been able to serve effectively on boards of directors of the General Board of Discipleship and the General Council on Ministries, worked with other ethnic caucuses on projects, served on various committees, and done consultations with numerous groups and annual conferences. BMCR has given me visibility and voice throughout the church. I have received personal satisfaction while striving toward the larger vision of enhancement and uplifting of the organization that serves the larger Black American constituency.

The challenge that was present before that Negro delegation in 1968 in Cincinnati, Ohio, is ever present today for me. In its history, BMCR has
—worked toward racial inclusiveness within the denomination at every level;
—worked for the strengthening of Black local churches;
—been an educational/training vehicle for individuals;
—been an arena to vent our frustrations within the church system;
—played the all-too-important role of being a central place for fellowship.
Black Methodists for Church Renewal has been and continues to be the conscience of the whole Church.

CHAPTER 10

The Value of BMCR to Whites and Other Constituencies

Evelyn Fitzgerald

If there were no BMCR, my church would be like potato soup—bland and without color. Without BMCR's constant advocacy for twenty-five years, The United Methodist Church could not claim and be enriched by the diversity brought by African-American United Methodists. Why should a white United Methodist care about diversity—care whether BMCR exists or doesn't exist? Let me count the ways!

Out of the terrible darkness that was and is racism, BMCR brought to light what racism looked like in The United Methodist Church. It was not pretty. It still is not pretty. And worse, it is sinful! Twenty-five painful years later, BMCR continues to witness to us about our racism. Praise God!

The members of Black Methodists for Church Renewal care enough for this white North American dominated United Methodist Church to stay with it, to celebrate the small

victories, yet endure the agony of never reaching their ultimate goal of genuine racial inclusiveness. It is not that they do not have other options. They do. There are other options for them to remain in the Wesleyan tradition. Members of the African Methodist Episcopal, African Methodist Episcopal Zion, and Christian Methodist Episcopal churches do not understand why their United Methodist brothers and sisters would remain in a racist church rather than come home to a church of their own unique culture. African-American United Methodists frequently find themselves in a double bind where they have to defend their choice to be United Methodists with their African-American brothers and sisters on one hand, and confront the white racist church and its members on the other hand. African Americans pay a psychological and emotional price to exercise this choice. They pay that

The Ebony Bishops at 1988 General Conference. (standing, l. to r.) Felton E. May, Melvin G. Talbert, Edsel A. Ammons, F. Herbert Skeete, W. T. Handy, Jr., Ernest W. Newman, Woodie W. White. (front row, l. to r.) Edward G. Carroll, Noah W. Moore, Ernest T. Dixon, Jr., James S. Thomas, Leontine T. C. Kelly, Prince A. Taylor, Roy C. Nichols. Not present: Forrest C. Stith.

(PHOTO COURTESY OF JOHN COLEMAN)

price because they belong here, they call this church home, and they want to be United Methodists. I appreciate their willingness to pay this price. I want them here.

The high price in patience and courage that BMCR has paid quadrennium after quadrennium, however, has resulted in the presence of nine "Ebony Bishops" in the Council of Bishops. Praise God again! We cannot sing the praises of their presence and leadership in the Council enough. We cannot be grateful enough for their overall contributions, but especially mention the "Defense of Creation" study, the Bishop's Drug Initiative, the increased understanding of the role of the African nations in the global village, the Study of the Ministry, the eradication of racism, the development of racial ethnic minority local congregations, and so on.

The Ebony Bishops and the African-American clergy have shared their cultural worship style with the whole church, for which I am eternally grateful. BMCR has been a strong advocate in this regard, and without their advocacy my worship opportunities over the past two decades would have been severely limited. Bishop Leontine Kelly might have remained the Reverend Leontine Kelly, and I would not have had the joyful, celebrative Holy Communion service I was privileged to participate in under the leadership of this outstanding bishop. I would not know what worship could be like without the African-American clergy and churches. I would not know about call and response (now as a pastor I keep hoping it will break out in my white church!). I would not have the deep appreciation I now have for gospel music, not just its joy, but its theology, too. I would not know that Christians can be happy and joyful in Jesus, while a boot on a white foot rests on their necks, keeping them "in their place." I would not have known that Christians could have that kind of spirit!

Black Methodists for Church Renewal is a role model for other minority groups. White women are one of those groups. BMCR's acceptance of its role to change a racist-dominated church to a multi-cultural church has given courage and strength to other groups. It broke the hard core of resistance for the others. Its advocacy for a national agency to combat racism in the 1960s was successful. BMCR is the parent organization of the General Commission on Religion and Race. The establishment of this national commission in 1968 gave encouragement to women, primarily white women, to submit legislation for a similar commission to monitor the inclusion of women throughout The United Methodist Church. It, too, was successful, and so we have the General Commission on the Status and Role of Women. Following the example of

63

Religion and Race, Status and Role of Women successfully proposed goals for the inclusion of women at all levels of the Church. I helped fill the women's goal for Religion and Race in 1977. I smile when I realize who was my real benefactor.

At a deeply personal level, there are two significant thoughts I want to register in closing. First, if BMCR had not given birth to the General Commission on Religion and Race, I would never ever have had that most marvelous, unique experience, for a white person, of working for and with not only African-Americans, but other racial ethnic minority persons for so many years. To know so many persons different from myself was a radical, life-changing experience.

Second, I am sincerely appreciative for the number of members of Black Methodists for Church Renewal who love me enough to tell me about my sin of racism. They love me enough to tell me when my behavior is racist. They love me enough to share how being the recipient of my racism hurts and hinders them. Sometimes they tell me quietly, on the side; at other times they are so angry they cannot rein in their anger. They love me enough to let me experience their culture, to teach me what it means to be African-American in the United States and in The United Methodist Church. The love is reciprocal!

CHAPTER 11

A White Reporter Covers BMCR

Winston H. Taylor

It was a time when the rhetoric of Stokeley Carmichael, H. Rap Brown, and others had whites in The Methodist Church dismayed at best and scared at worst. In that atmosphere, the announcement of another national gathering of Negro Methodists made the white members either hopeful or more scared.

The Black Manifesto, "Black power," and "Black pride" were among the slogans in current use. When the 1968 organizing meeting of BMCR acted quickly to provide its own definition of "Black power," some of those fears were at least diffused.

That new definition was a "call for black people to unite, to recognize their heritage, to build a sense of community, to act in a responsible way to meet the problem of racism." BMCR's declaration that it was for "the good of the whole nation" and was not designed to be separatist cooled more fears.

Another term that provided tension was *caucus*, for there had been no use of that word among Methodists, even though power-seeking special-interest groups had abounded for years. *Caucus* was still a "dirty word" in many circles, evidence that something must be afoot.

Not all of the non-Black members or groups responded in the same ways to this new threat—or promise. For whites who had been supporting Black aspirations, it provided a new avenue of cooperation. It was a sign that Negro Methodists were not trying to respond in the "white way," and that could be either hopeful or alarming. Of course, a majority group seldom believes that a minority's ways of moving are proper or effective.

To other ethnic minority members in the Church, however, BMCR provided a model that most followed later in their own struggles for a larger share in the Church.

It was a sign that Black members were taking themselves to task, challenging themselves to help achieve what they had been demanding of the predominantly white church. One of the strongest examples of such challenges came from BMCR's president, Gilbert Caldwell, at its 1972 convention, when he accused Black leaders of failing to encourage young people to get full educations, of "playing games" with young people by imitating their language and life-styles. This was a criticism that both supportive and opposing whites could buy into. Such challenges also could be perceived positively or negatively.

The calls for Blacks to "contribute from their own faith and heritage" also were well received in non-Black communities.

One of the most promising aspects of BMCR to most white members was BMCR's expression of determination to "stay within the church" and not secede. Withdrawal would have meant not only a statistical loss but a severe loss in prestige—showing that the Church had not been able to achieve its stated goals.

Many whites in Methodism could feel and understand the Black disappointment that "integrated" conferences had failed to live up to the hopes for them. There already was frustration in both camps about misunderstandings over the differences between "deadline" and "goal" for integration. Consequently, BMCR's image among whites went in many directions, sometimes helpful and sometimes fearful.

Although it was often a touch-and-go experience, BMCR's masterful planning of the ring of people surrounding delegates to the 1970 General Conference, while presentations were made about ethnic minority hopes and needs, was probably the stroke that convinced the church generally that BMCR demonstrated responsibility.

One of the things helpful to this reporter was to sense that, when one BMCR speaker interrupted his address to call me a "honkey" and question my presence as a reporter-photographer, there were people and leaders in BMCR who had invited me, knew why I was there, and would support my relationship with them.

In retrospect, the formation of BMCR, at a time of harsh and violent confrontations in many interracial situations, helped United Methodists see the possibilities for peace and cooperation. It enabled whites to see Black people through another set of lenses.

CHAPTER 12

The Human Witness of BMCR

John W. Coleman, Jr.

During the 1991 annual meeting of Black Methodists for Church Renewal in Houston, Texas, I witnessed the ecstatic glow of discovery among a small group of members who had come from a church in Louisiana. Having just emerged from a workshop on getting more men involved in the local church, they discussed excitedly how they might use some of the ideas just presented in their congregation.

The scene reminded me of similar situations I had encountered during my four years at NOW newspaper, BMCR's publication that connects and informs thousands of members and numerous chapters across the United States. I was on staff 1981–85, first as an intern and then as editor, reporting on the activities and concerns of the caucus. Later, I volunteered to edit several issues while working with United Methodist Communications.

My tenure at NOW taught me much about the strength and vitality of the Black church in United Methodism. Most of all, I learned that the Black church is more than a monolithic institution and more than the selective memory of past glories. It is instead a richly human adventure, full of passion and purpose, of dreams and disappointments, giving birth to yet new dreams.

At national and jurisdictional annual meetings, youth conferences, and other BMCR special events, I was constantly moved by the eloquent, impassioned oratory; the enlightening workshops with insightful presentations and dialogue; and the soul-stirring worship services with powerful sermons and music. To experience these highlights was always fascinating and often exhilarating. And to report on them for NOW's readers was more a privilege than a duty. Indeed, I felt proud of my responsibility as I waded through precious notes and relived high moments on recorded tapes.

But the most gratifying experience was to witness the impact of those moments on participants: to look around and observe reactions to a rousing keynote address or sending-forth sermon; to overhear reflections and new ideas stimulated by workshops; and to later learn of churches and local caucuses putting those new ideas to good use. These outcomes assured me, thank God, that BMCR gatherings were not and are not static events that merely happen and then disappear into the dusty pages of unrecalled, useless history. I've heard of people who were inspired to pursue careers in ordained ministry and Christian education because their hearts were strangely warmed during a BMCR youth conference or annual meeting workshop. I've seen people virtually aflame as they departed from North Central Jurisdiction BMCR's awesome Convocation on Black Preaching and Worship in September 1982 and likewise from the Black Pentecost meeting in August 1988. And I've read of visionary attempts to replicate these and other events in local church, conference, and jurisdictional settings.

The human adventure of BMCR is the warm embrace of fellowship that fills hallways at annual meetings; the poignant expressions of pain and anger in response to injustice and institutional neglect; the community-building that undergirds the mutual search for solutions; the generosity of individuals, churches, and local caucuses that faithfully support what they proudly claim as their caucus, their voice in a predominantly white and often insensitive denomination; and the leaders at all levels of the Church who have the opportunity to make decisions about programs and policies largely because of BMCR's struggles to recruit, train, nurture, and involve more African-American leadership in the Church.

I deeply appreciate the human dimensions of BMCR no less than the historic contributions that shape our legacy as an organization. While editor of NOW, I was fortunate to be able to chronicle the development of that legacy. And like so many others, I continue to benefit from it.

Deborah Bass. Black Pentecost, Atlanta, 1988.

(PHOTO COURTESY OF JOHN COLEMAN)

Black Pentecost, Atlanta, 1988.

(PHOTO COURTESY OF JOHN COLEMAN)

Bishop Forrest C. Stith. Black Pentecost, Atlanta, 1988.

(PHOTO COURTESY OF JOHN COLEMAN)

Bishop Roy C. Nichols. Black Pentecost, Atlanta, 1988.
(PHOTO COURTESY OF JOHN COLEMAN)

(l. to r.) Bishop W. T. Handy, Bishop Roy C. Nichols, Ethel Johnson, Ernest L. Swiggett, John C. Corry, Bishop Leontine T. C. Kelly. Black Pentecost, Atlanta, 1988.

(PHOTO COURTESY OF JOHN COLEMAN)

CHAPTER 13

The United Methodist Church's View of the Significance of BMCR

Barbara Ricks Thompson

"Suppose the whole body were an eye—then how would you hear? Or if your whole body were just one big ear, how could you smell anything?" (I Corinthians 12:17, *The Living Bible*).

Suppose the membership of The United Methodist Church consisted of only white persons—then how would it reflect the genius and beauty of God's creation? Or if the *United Methodist Hymnal* and *Book of Worship* reflected only a European heritage—how would we know the richness of the cultures of our global community?

To understand the significance to The United Methodist Church of Black Methodists for Church Renewal (BMCR) is to comprehend the unsuppressible sense of fulfillment that comes with each small accomplishment and each measure of progress in overcoming racism.

Is it realistic to assume that The United Methodist Church is able to articulate the true significance of BMCR in its life? Is it realistic to assume that the "sinner" is able to step back from sinning and to appreciate those who call the sin by its name—racism?

BMCR is both a visible part and a not very visible part of the experience that has helped to bring to the denomination an improved measure of the racial and ethnic minority inclusiveness that is present today in the body United Methodist.

BMCR's visibility was most electric in the late 1960s, when the denomination was confronted with the challenge that no longer would it be acceptable to be the taillight, reflecting whence society had moved. United Methodism had to become a headlight and, by example, provide leadership to society in addressing the systemic racism that pervaded the institutions of the United States. Black people were tired of waiting for the "just love everybody" theology to inspire the white members of the denomination to experience transformation from being participants in the perpetration of racism to being the embodiment of community. The Church had to be *renewed*.

There is a paradigm for BMCR's ministry of calling the Church to task. The radical teachings of Jesus Christ disrupted the comfortable way things were with the Pharisees and the Sadducees and set in motion a new mandate for living and relating as people of God. BMCR's continual holding forth of the manifestations of racism within the Church is evidence of the caucus's loving belief that *renewal* of the Church is possible.

The efforts of BMCR help the denomination increase the participation of its Black members in decision-making places within the Church. The whole Church benefits from the more inclusive program development and delivery that occurs through annual conferences and general agencies.

Local communities and congregations are culturally and spiritually richer when they have experienced the ministry of Black pastors.

Some congregations have been forced to confront their own racism when Black pastors appointed to predominantly white congregations have been subjected to racial harassment and abuse. Some of the congregations have known *renewal* as they have responded in the spirit of shalom. (Unfortunately, some others have strayed away from their Christian heritage and joined in to be a part of the abusive community.)

Another vital contribution the denomination receives from BMCR is the nurturing environment it provides to Black members when the oppressiveness of racial harassment, prejudice, and discrimination become overwhelming. BMCR is a haven when one must weigh the ambiguity of love for the community of faith known as The United Methodist Church against the assault on integrity of personhood and cultural heritage. This haven *renews* the strength of Black members to continue in the struggle that brings wholeness to the denomination and affirmation for themselves. Black Methodists for Church Renewal is a gift, a sign of grace, for The United Methodist Church.

CHAPTER 14

A Reminder
of the Church's Diversity

Joseph Roberson

The perennial questions that face me, in numerous places, are: Why do we need BMCR? and Why do Black Methodists need a caucus in an inclusive United Methodist Church? These questions are raised because many persons believe that the Commission on Religion and Race, an outgrowth of BMCR, and the Ethnic Local Church Concerns Committee are adequate to address the concerns of Blacks and other racial ethnic groups. I greatly appreciate the efforts and objectives of both groups. They have a necessary role and have a correlative relationship with BMCR and other caucuses. However, one must always realize that their role is often influenced and sometimes restricted by the majority white constituency, which controls funds and recommendations for these groups.

BMCR, as an independent caucus body, can legitimately serve as the prophetic and political voice for Black Methodists. BMCR is called to be the conscience of The United Methodist Church and maintains a prophetic witness to the Church and to the world. Consequently, the new self-esteem of belonging to "the whole" United Methodist Church does not mean a loss of one's identity in the Black church and the Black community. To be in Christ means to be free in an inclusive Church.

The relevancy of BMCR helps the Church reclaim its soul from the atrocities of racism and bigotry. Otherwise the Church could be consumed by the ills of the secular society.

BMCR is a recognizably important entity within the Church and continues with the same focus established at its Organizing National Conference in Cincinnati in 1968. The focus was then, as it is now, a demand for *self-definition*, *self-determination*, and *Black solidarity*.

Self-definition

Professor James H. Cone, author of *Black Theology and Black Power*, states in his book: "God's words of reconciliation mean that we can only be justified by becoming black. Through this radical change we become identified totally with the black masses." Professor Cone intimates that being Black in America is not exclusively a matter of skin color. He says, "You can be black and not be committed to the liberation of black people."

BMCR continues to perpetuate the awareness of the history, heritage, and contributions of African-American Methodists. Such contributions remain virtually an untold story. Only recently have major books and writings revealed such figures as Harry Hosier, Henry Evans, the Unknown Betty, and the struggles of the Central Jurisdiction. Our story and heritage began with the introduction of Methodism into the American Colonies and continues into the twenty-first century.

Self-determination— Strengthening the Black Church

BMCR is needed to strengthen the Black church for the twenty-first century with serious attention being given to congregational development, leadership development, ministerial recruitment, outreach, and youth/ young adult ministries. A view of Black United Methodist membership data, 1964–1991, raises some questions about a problematic

decline in membership. In 1964, the Central Jurisdiction recorded 373,595 black members; in 1968, 385,000; and in 1991, approximately 275,000 members. In 1964 we had 2,853 Black churches, and in 1991 we had 2,425. In my opinion Black church development, in most annual conferences, is not a high priority of The United Methodist Church. In recent years, more attention has been given to the start of congregations in the white, Korean, and Hispanic communities, but little attention has been given to the Black communities. The role of BMCR is to help develop and demand of The United Methodist Church an African-American church development plan.

Black churches that are experiencing serious membership growth are focusing upon recovering our spiritual roots and self-determination. BMCR dispels the concept that Black people can succeed in the Church only if they are shaped in the image of white, middle-class pseudo-sophisticates.

Jurisdictional caucuses are becoming more active and effective in shaping episcopal elections. Notice should be made that while BMCR has been highly visible in the episcopal election process, it is concerned that there are six active female bishops but no Black female bishops. The first and only Black female to be elected to date was Leontine Kelly in 1984. Three Blacks were elected this quadrennium: Alfred Norris, Charles Jordan, and William Morris.

Installation of officers, 1984. (l. to r.) Bishop James S. Thomas, Betty Henderson, John G. Corry, Henry Wilkins, Ernest L. Swiggett. (PHOTO COURTESY OF NATIONAL BMCR, DAYTON)

Black Solidarity

BMCR is a vital link in the encouragement of solidarity among Black United Methodists. The foundation of racial solidarity is not the family but the church. Our families were almost destroyed in slavery. Our mothers and fathers, sisters and brothers were sold from plantation to plantation, our businesses were crushed, our schools disallowed; only the Black church endured. The fight for freedom is still the burden of the Black church and BMCR. Martin Luther King, Jr., once said, "The world is being destroyed not so much by the words of bad people as by the appalling silence of good people." Through the church and BMCR we have the opportunity to speak out boldly for freedom and justice.

The National BMCR annual meeting is a significant opportunity for unity, fellowship, spiritual renewal, and leadership training. BMCR has cultivated and nurtured leadership for the entire Church. This process is self-defining at its best. We have launched persons in the Church from the district to the general Church levels.

In conclusion, the need for BMCR continues because justice, identity, solidarity, and self-determination demand a responsive voice. *Now is the time!*

79

CHAPTER 15

Why Do We Still Need BMCR?

Ernest L. Swiggett

Given the social and political fabric of the environment in which we live, one can get slightly petulant or even bemused when asked: Why do we need BMCR? One experiences a similar reaction when queried: Why do we need the historic Black United Methodist Colleges—or civil rights organizations or any entity that advocates for the rights of its constituents?

The first response to that initial question is quite simple. We need BMCR because racism is still rampant in the land. And since The United Methodist Church often mirrors the larger universe, it is impossible to condemn racism in the universe without boldly confronting racism in The United Methodist Church.

BMCR was called into being to thwart racism within the "new" United Methodist Church. Two of its purposes are to expose racism wherever it raises its ugly head and to vigilantly sensitize United Methodist boards and agencies to be inclusive and relevant. Yes, persons can quip, there is an "increase." There are Ebony Bishops, Black district superintendents and board and agency secretaries and directors, and some meaningful cross-racial appointments. However, when you lift the covers, the snake of racism is coiled ready to spring into action. The mobility of Blacks within the Church is often through a forced selection rather than a natural one since Blacks are still measured by the color of their skin instead of the contents of their minds.

These purposes are carried out through the political agenda of BMCR. As with any advocacy entity, BCMR has far greater latitude in addressing issues of racism and taking unpopular stands than individuals or agencies who might become victims of veiled repercussions.

Negail Riley, keynote speaker. Fifteenth annual meeting, St. Louis, 1982.

(PHOTO COURTESY OF NATIONAL BMCR, DAYTON)

In affirming individual worth and value, BMCR cultivates, nurtures, and supports laity and clergy to be witnesses in this Church by helping them learn what United Methodism is, what is its structure, how boards and agencies function in mission, what connectionality is, and how not to be destroyed by the system. These issues are dealt with through all levels, from the local church to the national office.

For almost twenty-five years, Black persons have gathered at BMCR's Annual Meeting from across the Church to be with one another, to affirm who we are and whose we are, to sing the songs of Zion, and to be empowered by the Word. There is no other gathering as unique in addressing and responding to these sociospiritual needs. It often eases the pain of racism and even propels us back into the fray.

These are the paramount reasons for the existence of BMCR. And until justice flows righteously from pew to pew, from pulpit to pulpit, and until the church is not the most segregated assembly on Sunday morning, there will always be a need for BMCR. And if it didn't exist, the tenor and horror of these days would demand its creation.

CHAPTER 16   A New Beginning

Bishop Roy C. Nichols

A feeling of unease was widespread when Methodism's General Conference convened in Dallas, Texas, April 23, 1968. Martin Luther King, Jr., had been assassinated on the back porch of a little Memphis motel, on April 4. A few weeks after adjournment, on June 5, Robert Kennedy was gunned down in the kitchen of a Los Angeles hotel. Racism was at the root of both acts of violence. That was the year BMCR was born.

Black Methodists for Church Renewal came into being twenty-five years ago to eradicate racism within The United Methodist Church. The racial composition of the Church has changed significantly since 1968. Korean congregations are growing at the fastest rate. Southeast Asian, Pacific Islander, and Hispanic congregations are also on the increase. In recent years, however, Black Methodists have begun to follow the downward membership spiral of the general Church. It is clear, therefore, that while BMCR must continue to monitor the UMC's racial practices, this task must be shared with other racial minorities within the Church. At the same time, our focus must continue to shift in the direction of local church growth and congregation revitalization.

My recent book, entitled *Doing the Gospel*, offers some helpful suggestions. It includes brief descriptions of 140 local churches of different races and sizes, attracting and serving the needs of more and more people. In the second section of the book, there is an anatomically designed programmatic pattern for ministry. African-American congregations, however, must provide an additional programmatic ingredient addressed to our peculiar need.

Because our record of achievement and contribution has been ignored in America's educational menu, our congregations need to be taught more about our history, beginning with Africa, the homeland of human civilization. We need to know the names and deeds of the great women and men who are a part of our past and present. This educational adventure must be more than occasional insertions in a sermon. We need regular classes for all ages. We need a clear affirmation of our ownership in the USA, as well as our primary identity as children of God. BMCR must provide an agenda for the local churches to teach their congregations to wear our blackness with dignity and appropriate pride.

Mission and evangelism have always been the first priority of all true disciples of Jesus Christ. The former includes all that we do to serve the needs of others, in the name of Jesus Christ. The latter includes all that we do to acquaint others with the saving grace of God revealed in Jesus Christ.

United Methodism's newest missionary venture in the Third World is the establishment of Africa University in Zimbabwe. The campus will be dedicated on April 23, 1994. It will be a United Methodist first—a fully accredited, degree granting, church-related university for a continent of young Africans hungry for learning. BMCR must lead the list of supporters of this once-in-a-lifetime mission project.

Evangelism is every Christian's business. But because we are who we are and because of our traditional role in the Black community, we need to redefine ourselves to become "Saving Stations," gateways into the kingdom of God, ministering to the total needs of the people. By the grace of God, through BMCR we can experience resurrection in the Black community right now!

BMCR's future agenda must also include building bridges of understanding and cooperation between and among all races and cultures. Our difficult struggle against racism in America should make us ardent apostles of interracial and intercultural accord. African, Asian, European, and Hispanic Americans have a divine assignment: to prove to the world that multi-colored and multi-cultured people can dwell together in peace, contributing to the prosperity and security of each other: "One nation, under God, with liberty and justice for all."

Having lived through America's involvement in seven wars, the Great Depression of the 1930s, the long years of legalized racism and lynching, the turbulent civil rights revolution of the 1940s, 50s, and 60s, and the last twelve years of "benign neglect," I am feeling optimistic about the future. In the public sector we now have a President who talks about "putting people first." Big business is beginning to realize that America's racial diversity is an asset, not a liability.

Workshop led by Walter Kimbrough. Annual meeting, Oakland.

(PHOTO COURTESY OF JOHN COLEMAN)

In the UMC, two-thirds of our episcopal leadership has changed in the last eight years. The laity is expectant. Children and youth are ready to exchange destructive guns, drugs, and a reckless sex culture for new ways of pursuing "life, liberty, and happiness." Anointed, prepared, pastoral leadership, anxious to do the will of God, is all that is needed to precipitate a new kind of comprehensive revival that will transform our conventional congregations into dynamic mission movements.

God has gifted each of us with intelligence, imagination, and endurance. Without these qualities, we would not have survived. So, in the modified words of the Great Apostle:

Let us move everything that is
   blocking our path,
forsaking the sins that destroy
   our bodies, minds, and souls;
Taking hold of the opportunities for which
   so many have struggled so hard
    to obtain
And make haste, in the right direction,
Always depending on the power of God
   revealed in Jesus Christ our Lord,
Who inspires and liberates
   true believers who are willing to
   work out their salvation.

CHAPTER 17

The Future—What Now?

Tallulah Williams

"I will sing a new song. As difficult as it is, I must learn the new song that is capable of meeting the new need. I must fashion new words born of all the new growth of my life, my mind, and my spirit. I must prepare for new melodies that have never been mine before, that all that is within me may lift my voice unto God. How I love the old familiarity of the wearied melody—how I shrink from the harsh discords of the new untried harmonies. But I will sing, this day, a new song unto Thee, O God."

Howard Thurman, **Meditations of the Heart**

Since its inception, Black Methodists for Church Renewal has been the voice of the Black church and an advocate for its growth and development. It has been instrumental in creating agencies and programs in the general Church. Much of the organization's efforts have been focused on the mandate of renewing The United Methodist Church by witnessing, advocating, networking, and strategizing for creative change. The history of the BMCR demonstrates its resilience, its creativity, its enduring resources, and its sense of hope.

BMCR's full potential has not been realized, and its efforts are still needed today. BMCR has made great strides, but the struggle has not been won. BMCR must seek answers to the serious challenges posed by the changing circumstances of our times. Racial hatred and psychological oppression are the order of the day. We live in a time when persons are judged by the color of their skin rather than the content of their character. Economic oppression continues to separate the haves from the have-nots. Persons in the Black community are looking for a way out of powerlessness and hopelessness, only to become more shackled by the chains of dope, alcohol, violence, and crime. Homelessness, mental illness, poverty, and hunger are rampant. Unemployment is at an all-

Ernest A. Smith, whose cry, "Our time under God is now!" became the BMCR motto.
(RALPH W. ARMSTRONG PHOTOGRAPHY; PHOTO COURTESY OF NATIONAL BMCR, DAYTON)

time high. The fiber of the Black family is unraveling. There is little self-dignity and self-respect in our children, who, following their adult role models, hustle nickels and dimes to buy a hamburger. AIDS is murdering our future. There are more than 900,000 Black men in prison. Black life is cheap. And there is silence!

Our society and our denomination for far too long have committed the grievous sin of being comfortable while dignity was being stripped from God's people. BMCR has also been plagued by a spirit of apathy and complacency. The organization has lost its zeal to be a prophetic and explosive power.

It was a rather embarrassing question that God put to Elijah one day when he asked, "What are you doing here, Elijah?" Elijah was whining and complaining and wishing he were dead. In his lifetime he had achieved many victories, but then came the realization that these victories were only memories. Today, God poses similar questions to BMCR. BMCR, what are you doing? What contributions are you making in the lives of the Black community, the Black church, The United Methodist Church, and the world? BMCR, are you giving your best in the service of the Lord?

Today and toward the future, BMCR faces a great challenge of responsibility in the empowerment of Black Methodists for effective wit-

ness and service. BMCR must equip leadership and strengthen local churches for powerful evangelism, committed stewardship, and effective outreach. The survival tactics of the past are no longer appropriate for the hopelessness of the present. What is needed today is a spiritual awakening to provide a moral and spiritual dynamic to change situations and enhance the quality of life. Hence, BMCR must be all it can be as an instrument of God's transforming spirit. BMCR must address this new sense of urgency.

BMCR must live out God's message of salvation and liberation by example. It must not only point the way to hope, it must lead in the direction of hope. The organization can do this only as we claim what is ours. BMCR must take control of its own destiny. It must become financially solvent, with the knowledge that people support what they believe in. The focus must move from passive internal action to aggressive external action.

Black Methodists possess the greatest wealth of programming resources. Visions and directions have been strategized and developed by Ebony Bishops, boards of directors, blue ribbon committees, general Church staff, Black district superintendents, local churches, clergy, and laity. It is now time for action. BMCR's rhetoric must now be brought to life. BMCR must continue in tooling the Black constituency for action in the strengthening of local churches, local BMCR caucuses, and annual conferences. BMCR must seriously challenge and confront racism. BMCR is mandated by the gospel to fight for justice and liberation. BMCR must become hope for the Black community. BMCR must become hope for Black Methodists. BMCR must become hope for The United Methodist Church.

The challenge is clear, the opportunity is near, and the time to act is now. "From this day forward, our dedication must be deep, our commitment sure, and our action certain. God's work and way are contemporary in every age. There is no waiting for tomorrow. . . . Our time under God is now!" (Dr. Ernest A. Smith).

"Sing a song full of the faith that the
    dark past has taught us,
Sing a song full of the hope that the
    present has brought us;
Facing the rising sun of the new day
    begun,
Let us march on till victory is won."

James Weldon Johnson,
"Lift Every Voice and Sing"